RUSSIA-UKRAINE WAR: THE KISSINGER WAY TO END THE WAR?

AN EXPLANATORY REVIEW OF CONTEXT AND HISTORY

DR. PHILIP K. JASSEN

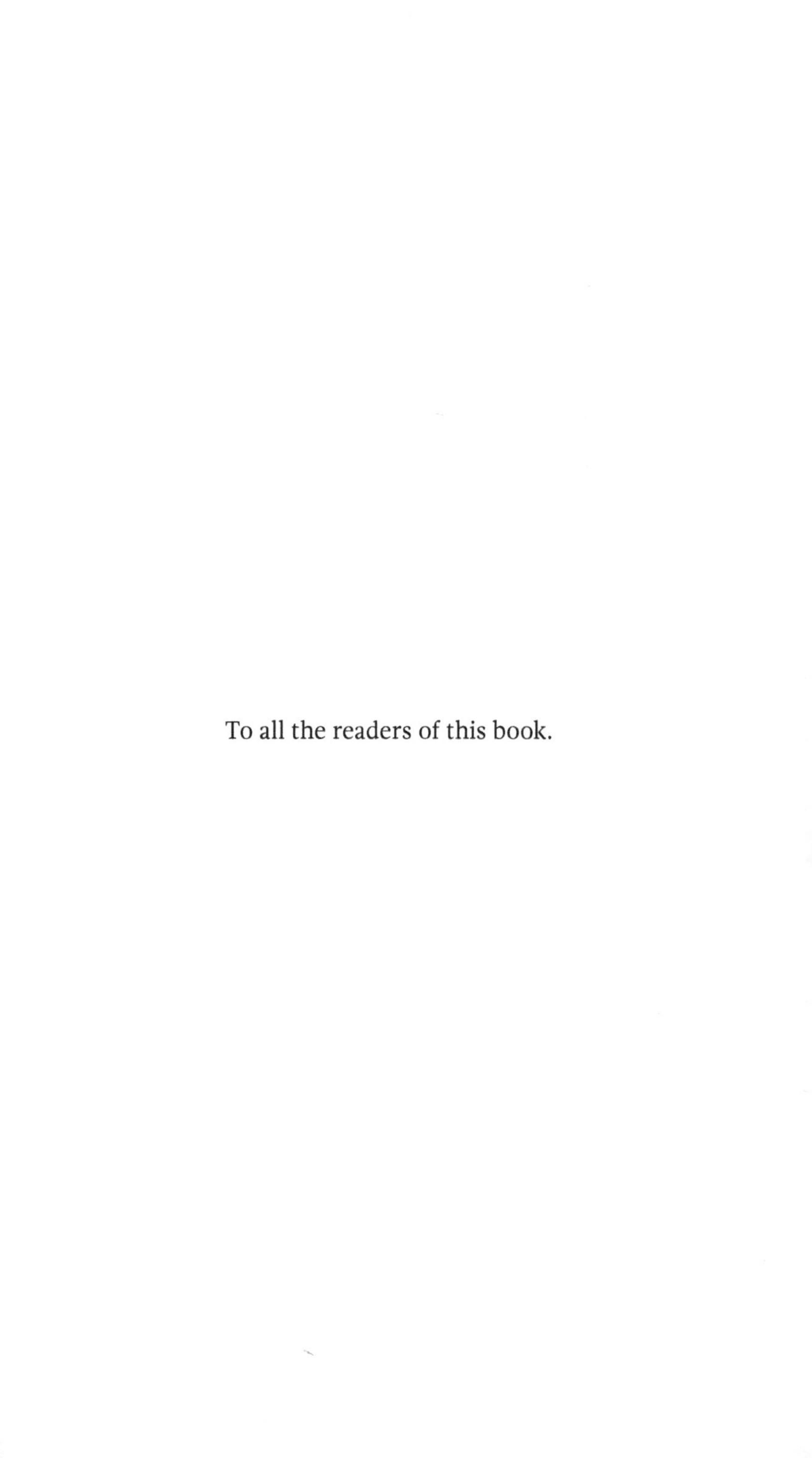

To all the readers of this book.

Contents

Foreword

The war of Ukraine has crossed over hundred days and still it is going and spilling blood over Ukraine. Probably Putin has gained confidence after encroaching Crimea in 2014 and after seeing the robotic inaction of the European powers, led by America. But this time, USA has perhaps understood its fault and it would not play the act of pre world war Britain.

But this war is taxing heavily on the world, to all the population. It is now needed urgently to end this bloodshed. But how? How this impossible can be possible?

This book tries to throw a glance over this issue, while keeping the records of context and history in its place.

Preface

War is ongoing. Russia and Ukraine, the erstwhile countrymen of Soviet are fighting to the utmost. But it must end for the betterment of the world. But how? How the adamant nations can be stopped over this issue to a honourable solution?

But possibly there is no possible honorable solution for this. But even, what can be a possible acceptable solution?

Acknowledgements

To my teachers, I owe everything.

Prologue

History, context and possibility of solution of Russia Ukraie
war.

CHAPTER ONE

ENDING UKRAINE WAR: THE KISSINGER FORMULA?

Former United States Secretary of State Henry Kissinger recently said that Ukraine must leave its territory to negotiate with Russia. His advice was blown out of proportion by Ukrainian President Volodymyr Zelensky. Now, with Kissinger's formula, there is a possibility of peace talks between the two countries. The United States has shown interest in resolving the crisis. Russian forces now control more than two-thirds of the eastern Ukrainian capital, Severodonetsk. With fierce street fighting in the city, Western officials say the Russian army's next target is the city of Sevyansk. Russia is now in a favorable position in the Ukraine campaign. US President Biden has also moved away from his previous position, pushing for a negotiated solution. In this context, Russia has also stated that it is ready for talks. Confirming the latest gains in Severodonetsk, a strategically important city east of Ukraine, Luhansk regional governor Serhi Haidai said on Wednesday that Russia controlled 80 percent of the city. "Unfortunately, today, Russian troops control most of the city," Haidai said. "Some Ukrainian troops have returned to more convenient, pre-prepared positions." US wants Russia-Ukraine talks to soften tone: With war escalating in Eastern Europe, the United States has stepped up support for Italy's peace plan for Ukraine. Speaking at a news conference on Tuesday, US Ambassador to the United Nations Linda Thomas-Greenfield said Washington supports all efforts to find a peaceful solution to the existing Ukrainian crisis. 'We encourage all efforts to find a peaceful solution for the Ukrainian people that is acceptable to them. And the Italian proposal is one of the initiatives we must take to see the conclusion of this horrific war and the horrific attack on Ukraine. " According to the report, Italy has submitted a four-point peace plan to UN Secretary General Antonio Guterres to resolve the ongoing war in Ukraine. The plan calls for a local ceasefire to allow a smooth path for civilians to evacuate and to create an environment for a comprehensive ceasefire that would lead to long-term peace in Ukraine. However, the Russian government has criticized Italy's peace plan, calling it "non-serious." Earlier, on May 26, Russian Foreign Minister Sergei Lavrov claimed that the proponents of the peace plan had no knowledge of the history of the ongoing crisis in Ukraine. Ukraine will lose Donbass 'in days or weeks': Retired German General Roland Ketter believes that Ukraine will lose control of the whole Donbass in days or weeks. 'I have an idea that Russia has changed its strategy in the last few days and weeks. They set a clear goal in Donbass and deployed their forces there, "said Cater. He stressed that the Russian armed forces are now significantly ahead of the Ukrainian army, which has virtually voluntarily left Kiev. Because, they have no interest there. Putin's promise to make Russia stronger: Russia will build its strength and sovereignty in a rapidly changing world, President Vladimir Putin said in a video speech on the International Day for the Protection of Children, which was screened at the Bolshoi Theater event on Wednesday. Putin congratulated parents, teachers and students. 'You are living and growing in a very dynamic time when the world is changing, and it is changing rapidly. I am convinced that in this complex world, Russia will only strengthen its power, independence and sovereignty, "Putin assured.

Russia's Defense Ministry spokesman Maj. Gen. Igor Konashenkov said yesterday that Russia's air defense forces had fired a Ukrainian SU-25 Ground Attack Plane near the

Donetsk People's Republic. Also, the Russian Air Defense Forces intercepted two Ukrainian rockets of the Smarch Multiple Launch Rocket System on the Malaya Kamishevakha and Kamenka settlements in the Kharkov region, the general said. The Russian air defense capabilities were carried out by seven Ukrainian drones near the Donetsk People's Republic's Gorlovka, Golmovsky, Yasinovataya and Vervarva, Malia Prokhodi and Novaya Ganilitsa in the Kharkov region, and the Pyatikhatkar community in the Kherson region. Russia ready to make peace: Russia is open to negotiations with Ukraine and the signing of an agreement that will lead to peace, Valentina Matvienko, speaker of the Russian Federation Council (upper house of parliament), said in a meeting with Mozambican President Felipe Nussi on Tuesday. "We are open to discussion. I fully share your position that a diplomatic, peaceful solution is needed. But it requires the will of both parties. We reiterate that we are ready for talks, but we do not see any response from Kiev, "he said. "Unfortunately, we did not get enough response," he said. And when Ukraine said they wanted to be a nuclear power and when we saw how aggressive they were A flood of weapons, I know they are planning a third armed attack on Donetsk. And in the Luhansk region, naturally, we had no other choice, no other option to ensure our safety. " Pushing citizens to death, DPR wants to try Zelensky: DPRK He has killed his countrymen in the interests of America. That is why the Donetsk People's Republic (DPR) wants to try him. In an interview with Newsmax television on Tuesday, Zelensky himself acknowledged that about 80 to 100 people in Ukraine's armed forces are dying every day. More than 500 are being injured. Although the UN is saying that the actual number is actually much higher. So the question is, knowing that so many soldiers are being killed, why is he forcing ordinary people to fight? By the way, military training is compulsory for everyone in Ukraine. Since the beginning of the Russian campaign, young people as well as the elderly and even minors have been forcibly recruited into the military. At the same time, schools in the city are practicing bombing or airstrikes. According to the BBC, even pensioners are being forced to attend weekend exercises in the woods outside Kiev. Experts believe that Zelensky is working as an American sportsman. Since coming to power, Biden has had to deal with two superpowers, China and Russia. The task is very difficult for the United States alone. As a result, he used Ukraine to suppress Russia so that he could gain European support. Biden himself has admitted that his goal is to cripple Russia so that it can no longer stand on its own two feet. He also called for the ouster of Putin. It was at his instigation that Zelensky became embroiled in a war with Russia, which was much stronger than Ukraine. Whatever the Russia-US victory or defeat, Ukraine is doomed. Asenier, a lawmaker from the Donetsk People's Republic, said on Wednesday that the Russian-backed region wanted to try Ukrainian President Zelensky as a war criminal. Speaking to Russia's state news agency Tas, Yelena Shishkina said the DPR would file charges against lawmakers who have led Ukraine since 2014, when Russian President Putin annexed Crimea. Among them are Zelensky, former acting president Oleksandr Turchynov, and former president Petro Poroshenko. NATO launches 'Third World War':

A prominent Russian state television presenter claims that World War III has already begun because of Western support for Ukraine's weapons. Russia 1 TV presenter Olga

Skabeva says Russia's so-called special military operation in Ukraine is over and "a real war has begun, World War III." He added that Moscow now needs to expand its goal of "demilitarization" to cover NATO countries. In Monday's 60-minute version of her program, Skabeva said, "It is time to acknowledge that, perhaps, Russia's special operation in Ukraine is now over, in the sense that a real war has begun, World War III."

CHAPTER TWO

Russian President Vladimir Putin

Russian President Vladimir Putin has warned Moscow that it will change its target if the West does not stop supplying missiles to Ukraine. "Weapons are being sent to Kiev to escalate the conflict," he said. Putin told the Russian news agency that if Western powers sent one long-range missile after another to Kiev in this way, we would justify it ... we would use our weapons. I will hit all the places where I have not attacked yet. 'This interview was shown on Russian television. Putin did not say where he was planning to attack. The United States has recently announced that it will launch a medium-range multiple rocket launch system. It can hit a target at a distance of 60 km. In addition, the United States is providing billions of dollars in weapons. Russia is angry at this. This means that this time Kiev's forces will be able to attack Russia from Ukraine. US President Joe Biden has said he will not give Ukraine any weapons that could cause damage to Russian territory. But neither side in the war trusts anyone. Putin, however, said the United States was not providing any new weapons to Ukraine. Ukraine also had such weapons made in the Soviet era. ' "The system that the United States is sending uses missiles with a range of 45-60 kilometers," he said. It is nothing. Their real purpose is to prolong the war. "

100 DAYS OF WAR: KIEV ELUSIVE TO RUSSIA CLAIMS ZELENSKY

Russia's dream of occupying Kiev has been shattered by Ukrainian forces. Russia now occupies the Donbass region of eastern Ukraine, which is largely inhabited by separatists. Today is the 100th day of the Ukraine-Russia war. Moscow declared war on Kiev on February 24. Where exactly is the situation today after 100 days? How successful has Russia been in aggression? What is Ukraine saying? Russia has occupied at least 20 percent of Ukraine in 100 days. This was stated yesterday by the President of Ukraine Volodymyr Zelensky. However, the Ukrainian army's dream of capturing the Russian capital Kiev has been shattered by Ukrainian forces. Russia now occupies the Donbass region of eastern Ukraine, which is largely inhabited by separatists. Moscow has begun trying to run a parallel regime there. That said, they have not stopped firing on Ukraine or launching missiles. Although the intensity of the attack has decreased, the shelling continues. NATO chief Jens Stoltenberg met with US President Joe Biden yesterday. He told Biden that the effects of the protracted war were being felt in Ukraine's neighbors. You have to stand by their side. "Thousands of people have been forced to flee Ukraine in the last 100 days," Zelensky said during a virtual administrative meeting with Luxembourg yesterday. Russian troops have killed scores of Ukrainian soldiers as well as scores of people. They have taken over at least 20 percent of our country, "he said. The strategic location of Severodnesk is very important. The Azat factory here is known as the largest chemical factory in Europe. The Russian army also attacked the factory's administrative building. However, Luhansk Governor Sergei Gade said the Ukrainian army was fighting through everything. They will not leave without seeing the end. On the other hand, Russia has started war crimes trials along with Ukraine. In some such cases, Moscow has been accused of "forcing" children from Ukraine to "ship" to Russia. General Irina Benedictova, who is in charge of investigating multiple war crimes in Ukraine, said that in the last 100 days since the start of the war, more than 20 cases have been filed in Russia for "trafficking" children from various Eastern European countries. He said that a case was being filed against the Russian prisoner of war for violating international war laws, killing innocent civilians without provocation, and genocide.

CHAPTER FOUR

PUTIN'S ARMY CAPTURES 200,000 CHILDREN IN UKRAINE?

Putin and Zelensky

Putin's army captures 200,000 children in Ukraine Complaint Zelensky The war began on February 24 when Russian President Vladimir Putin announced a military operation in Ukraine. Thursday marks the 100th day of that war. On the 100th day of the war, Ukrainian President Volodymyr Zelensky accused the Russian army of abducting children. "As many as 200,000 Ukrainian children have been forcibly relocated to Russia since the start of the offensive in February," he said on Thursday. Russian President Vladimir Putin announced a military operation in Ukraine on February 24. Earlier, he announced the recognition of the Donetsk and Luhansk regions of Ukraine (collectively called Donbass) as independent states. Incidentally, in the fifth month of the war, Donbass was facing Russian aggression. Putin's forces have resumed operations with the help of pro-Moscow separatist groups. According to Western media reports, the Ukrainian army has been cornered in the Donbass area due to the Russian attack in the last few weeks. Under the circumstances, Zelensky sought long-range missiles from the United States. But the Joe Biden government has said it will not give Ukraine any missiles that could strike mainland Russia. However, Biden declined to comment on Wednesday, saying "this is a clear step in the right direction."

A Complete Separation between Moscow and Washington is Impossible

Joe Biden

A complete separation between Moscow and Washington is impossible: US Ambassador Moscow and Washington cannot be completely different, said John Sullivan, the US ambassador to Russia, in an interview with the news agency Tas. "We are never completely isolated," Sullivan said. We can't really sever diplomatic relations, and we can't just talk. After all, we sit next to each other at the UN Security Council in New York every day. In any case, it is better for us to talk to each other at the UN, at the Security Council. And we should have embassies. That's the decent thing to do, and it should end there. " "We should have embassies in Moscow and Washington, not just the Russian mission to the United Nations. I just think, in reality, we will never reach the level of complete isolation because we (the United Nations) have joined as permanent members of the Security Council. And after joining in this way we need to be involved with each other despite the many competitive issues. We see each other, talk and visit New York on a daily basis, "said Sullivan.

CHAPTER SIX

Biden assures Ukraine of medium-range missiles Zelensky wanted long-range missiles from the United States. But Biden changed his mind after warnings from Russian President Vladimir Putin. US President Joe Biden has changed his mind about providing military assistance to Ukraine. "We have decided to supply a limited number of medium-range missiles to Ukraine in response to their request," Biden said on Tuesday. However, we will not give Ukraine any missiles capable of launching an attack on

Russian territory. " In this situation, the President of Ukraine wanted a long-range missile from the United States. But Biden changed his mind after warnings from Russian President Vladimir Putin. The United States has provided the FGM-146 Javelin missile, the main weapon of the Ukrainian army, to repel Russian tank fleets after Putin's forces invaded Ukraine on February 24. Anti-aircraft Stringer missiles have also been provided. But at the request of the Zelensky government, Kiev has not yet been given a "multi-barrel rocket launcher" or a heavy missile.

CHAPTER SEVEN

Ukraine convicts two more Russian war criminals A Ukrainian court has sentenced a 21-year-old Russian tank commander to life in prison for killing an unarmed man in the first case. A Ukrainian court has sentenced two Russian prisoners of war to life in prison for war crimes. Alexander Bobikin and Alexander Ivanov were convicted of unprovoked shelling and assault in two Kharkiv villages early in the war. They have been sentenced to more than 11 years in prison. War crimes trials have recently begun in Ukraine. A Ukrainian court has sentenced a 21-year-old Russian tank commander to life in prison for killing an unarmed man in his first case last week. Today, two more Russian soldiers were sentenced by the court to life in prison for violating the rules of war. According to the source, the lawyer of the Russian army has applied for the reduction of the sentence. It has been claimed that they did that on the instructions of the authorities. On the other hand, the organization has stated that it will take a tougher stance against Russia at the European Union (EU) meeting in Brussels on Monday night. At the meeting, the two countries finally reached an agreement on stopping oil imports from Russia. Following the declaration of war against Ukraine, the EU decided to impose sanctions on the import of oil and natural gas from Russia to corner it economically. But it was not possible to fully implement it.

Russia supplies 25% of Europe's oil and 40% of its gas. Some countries, such as Hungary, which rely heavily on Russia for energy, did not agree at all. After lengthy negotiations, the group's leaders have finally decided to cut oil and gas imports from Russia by 90 percent in the next six months. Russia's permanent representative to the EU, Mikhail Ulyanov, tweeted in response to the decision, "Russia will find another buyer." It says it is rapidly sending 900 million euros in aid to war-torn Ukraine. The head of the organization, Charles Michel, has assured that European countries will continue to provide cash in this way in the coming days to boost Ukraine's economy. Germany has promised to stand by all Russian citizens who oppose the state's aggressive stance on Ukraine. Most of those citizens are victims of political violence, German Foreign Minister Nancy Fazer has said, adding that Germany has decided to simplify the permitting process for granting them asylum. For the past several days, Moscow has been trying to annex Georgia's separatist province of Ossetia. Ossetia's Russian-backed leader initially gave a positive signal to Moscow, but later changed his mind. He gave a hint but later changed his mind. He said they would take action on July 18. However, the organization has announced a sudden change of decision. On the other hand, the administrator of Sevirodnetsk claimed on Tuesday that a chemical plant in the city had been severely damaged in the Russian airstrikes. Toxic nitric gas is emanating from the destroyed factory. He posted pictures of the pink smoke floating over the city.